OCEAN ANIMALS

Drawing in Color

Table of Contents

Are you ready for Drawing In Color?

This book will teach you a simple step-by-step process of drawing. You will see how all images can be broken down into basic shapes. These shapes create the underlying form for the image. Once the form is developed, details like texture and expression lines are added to make the image more realistic.

When you are ready, continue to improve your drawing skills by sketching and coloring the illustrations and photographs included in the back of this book. Use the drawing grids to keep everything in correct proportion.

With these clear step-by-step instructions, you will learn how easy it is to draw any image you want!

Drawing begins with very simple shapes: geometric shapes and organic shapes. Geometric shapes such as the square, circle, and triangle, are known around the world so everyone can use them as a guide for drawing. They have uniform measurements and their shapes are not usually seen in nature. Organic shapes are fluid, loose, and found in nature: rocks, clouds, and leaves, for example.

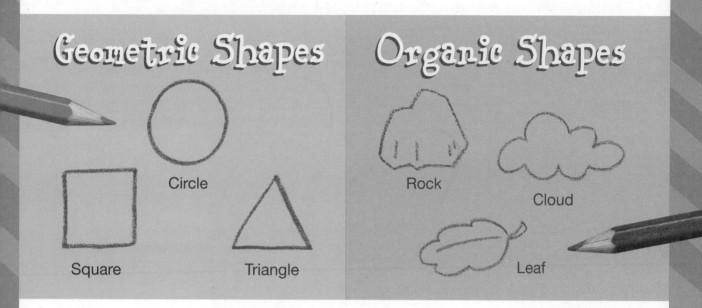

Geometric Shapes

Circle

Square

Triangle

Organic Shapes

Rock

Cloud

Leaf

With each of the animal drawings in this book, you will begin by drawing geometric shapes to create the basic figure. Then you will draw organic shapes to make the figure more natural. Next, you will develop texture and details by adding more organic shapes and lines. When you draw the details of the animal's face, remember that you are developing its emotional expression. Little changes in the eyes, nose, and mouth will bring a unique feeling to each drawing you create.

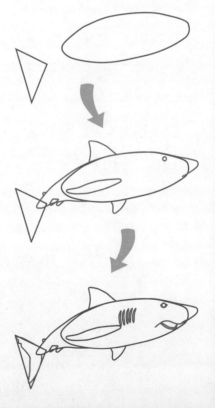

The Grid System

The step-by-step instructions include a visual aid tool called a grid, which is made up of either 9 or 12 squares. The grid is a guide that will help you draw correct proportions, which is the relationship between the size and location of the different parts of the animal.

In addition, four instruction grids are shown for each animal drawing. The first grid indicates where to place the basic geometric shapes. Grids for steps 2, 3 and 4 show the organic shapes, texture and details. The red lines in grids 1, 2, and 3 show the new lines you will draw in that step.

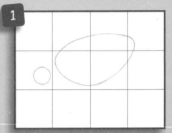

As you draw, look back and forth between the instruction grids and your drawing grid to see where the drawing lines meet or cross the grid lines. Try to focus on drawing one square at a time. The size and location of your lines will result in a realistically proportioned animal if you follow the proportions of the grid guide drawing. Changing proportions distorts or exaggerates features, which some artists do on purpose.

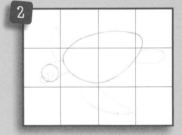

Now, let's learn drawing made easy!

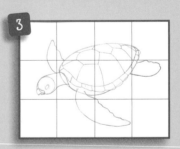

Coloring with Pencils

Add color to your drawing by starting out lightly and working up to darker shades.

Pressing down lightly   Pressing down hard

Build depth and texture into your sketches by blending and layering your colors for a painterly feel.

Here is the full spectrum of colors:

Dark Blue   Light Blue   Green   Yellow   Orange   Red   Violet

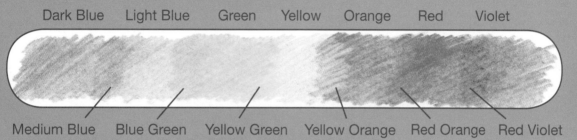

Medium Blue   Blue Green   Yellow Green   Yellow Orange   Red Orange   Red Violet

Let the white of the paper show through to bring highlights and light areas to your drawing.

Important Tips:

• You will need to sketch outlines before adding color. Use the drawing pencil included to make all the sketches.

• Before beginning to sketch, practice drawing circles, ovals, and lines on a sheet of paper. This will help you gain better control of your hand.

• Sketch the geometric shapes lightly. You will be drawing over them and erasing them as you finish your sketches.

• Mistakes are a natural and expected part of the drawing process, so keep your eraser handy!

• When adding color to your sketch, start off lightly. Note that colored pencil marks are difficult to erase.

• Keep drawing! The more you draw, the more your drawing skills will improve and your confidence as an artist will grow.

HOW TO DRAW A CRAB

Suggested colors:

1 Basic Shapes

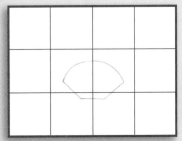

Before you begin, study the size and location of the shapes on the grid so that your proportions are correct. Start by drawing a fan or shell shape.

2 More Features

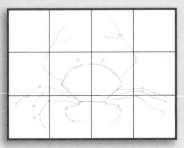

Draw a line for each eye stem. Draw a circle for each eye. Each leg will be drawn with several line segments. Draw a circle for every joint in each leg. Study the grid and the drawing to be sure you are including every joint. The claws are also drawn with basic lines at this point.

3 Adding Details

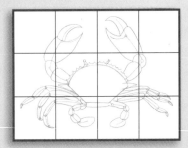

Time to draw organic shapes. Notice how these new lines are mostly curvy. Draw a scalloped line across the top of the fan shape. Draw a triangular shape on the outside edge of the fan to form another part of the crab shell. Draw curved lines to form the width of each crab leg segment. Draw a large curved and pointed shape for the top segments of each crab claw.

4 Finishing Touches

Erase the geometric shapes that remain visible. Now the crab is more lifelike because the organic shapes add form. Draw lines to form the width of the crab eyes. Draw two lines between the eyes to form two antennae. On the outlines for the claws, draw zigzag lines for the teeth on the crab claws. Add in additional short lines on the segments to add shape and depth to the body shell, legs, and claws.

TIP:

Place a sheet of paper under the side of your drawing hand as you sketch. This will keep your hand from smudging the pencil marks as you move along the paper surface.

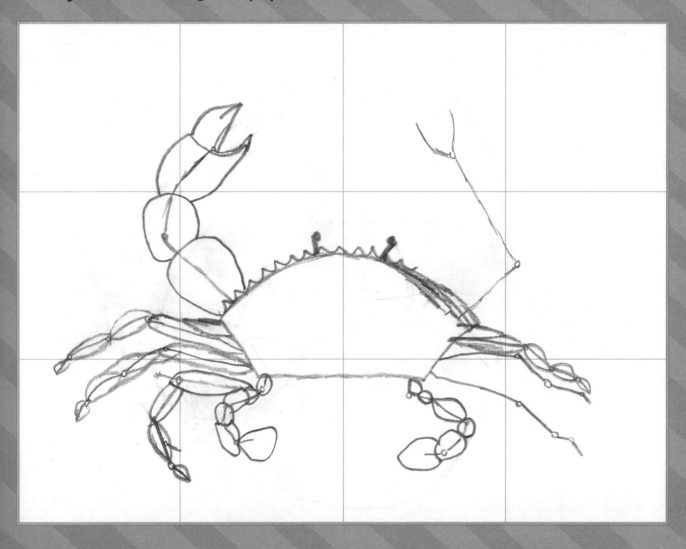

Did you know?

The giant spider crab is the world's largest crab, with a claw span of 8 to 9 feet (2.4 to 2.7 m).

HOW TO DRAW A SEAHORSE

Suggested colors: ● ● ● ● ● ●

1 Basic Shapes

Before you begin, study the size and location of the shapes on the grid so that your proportions are correct. Start by drawing circle for the seahorse head. Draw another circle for the body. Start by drawing a circle for the seahorse head. Draw another circle for the body. Draw a connecting line from the head to the body. Extend that line below the body circle for the tail.

2 More Features

Draw a small circle for the eye. Draw a longish rectangular shape for the snout. Draw a curved line to connect the head to the body to create the front of the neck and chest. Extend the line around the lower circle to form the belly. Continue the line and curl it at the end to form the shape of the tail.

3 Adding Details

Now, onto more organic shapes. These are all kinds of shapes. Draw a curved line for the cheek area. Draw the nostril. Draw lines to form a mane of narrow spines. Continue with a wavy line to form the back mane. Behind the belly circle, draw a small half-oval fin, with dots on the interior. Under the front belly, draw a small fin in a triangle shape.

4 Finishing Touches

Erase the geometric shapes that are visible. Now the seahorse is more lifelike because the organic shapes add form. To add texture and form, add many squarish-rectangular shapes along the length of the seahorse body. Draw the sea grass using long, thin lines. Add detail to the eye and face as shown. If you draw a larger pupil in the eye, it can completely change the expression on your seahorse's face. Try it!

Did you know?
Unlike any other species on Earth, the male seahorse becomes pregnant and gives birth instead of the female!

HOW TO DRAW A CLOWNFISH

Suggested colors:

1 Basic Shapes

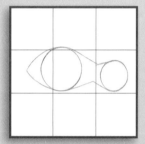

Start by drawing a large circle for the head area. Draw a smaller circle for the tail fin. Draw an angled line with a sharp break between the top of the head circle and the tail fin to form the back. Draw an angled line with a sharp break between the bottom of the head circle and the tail fin to form the belly. Draw an incomplete curved triangle with a point to form the front area of the fish's face.

2 More Features

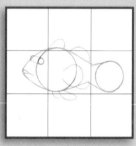

Draw a circle for the eyes. Extend that circle line through to where the eye would be on the other side of the fish's face. Draw two lines to form the mouth. Draw two half-circles to form the upper fins. Draw two half-ovals to form the lower fins; one is longer than the other. Draw a half-circle for the other lower fin. Draw an incomplete circle to form the side fin.

3 Adding Details

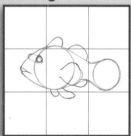

Time to draw organic shapes. Notice how these lines are uneven and curvy. They may be close to, or far away from, the geometric shapes. Draw small, wavy, almost zigzag lines, on the edges of the fins. Draw an inner circle for the eye.

4 Finishing Touches

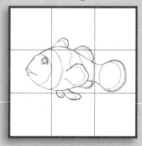

Erase the geometric shapes that remain visible. Now the clownfish is more lifelike because the organic shapes add form. Draw two smaller curved lines to finish forming the upper and lower lips. Add lines around the eye as shown. Draw additional lines to form the areas for the stripes on the body. Draw more wavy lines on the fins as shown to make the stripes on the fins.

Did you know?
Clownfish live within the venomous
tentacles of the sea anemone!

HOW TO DRAW A PENGUIN

Suggested colors: ● ● ● ●

1 Basic Shapes

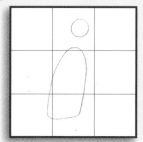

Before you begin drawing, pay attention to where both the oval and the circle shape are on the grid so that your proportions are correct. Start by drawing a large leaning oval with a flat bottom for the body. Next, draw a circle for the head.

2 More Features

Draw a circle for the eye. Draw an oval for the beak. Draw a connecting line between both the top and bottom of the head and the beak to form the rest of the head shape. Draw a connecting line between both the top and bottom of the head and the body to form the neck. Draw a curved line to form one edge of each wing. Draw a line for each leg. Draw an oval for each foot.

3 Adding Details

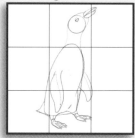

Time to draw organic shapes. Notice how these lines are uneven and curvy. They may be close to, or far away from, the geometric shapes. Draw a line for the eyelid. Draw lines to form the inner part of the beak. Draw a triangular shape to form the back tail feathers at the bottom of the body. Draw lines to form the width of the wings and the legs. Draw long toes with claws on the feet.

4 Finishing Touches

Erase the geometric shapes that remain visible. Now the penguin is more lifelike because the organic shapes add form. To add a feathery texture, draw many short lines in the outline of the tail feathers and lower body. Draw webbing between the toes. Draw uneven lines on the face and body to show the areas where the colors change from black to white.

Did you know?

The emperor penguin can stay underwater without breathing for 18 minutes!

HOW TO DRAW A WALRUS

Suggested colors:

1 Basic Shapes

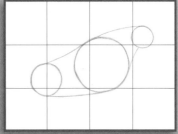

Before you begin, study the size and location of the shapes on the grid so that your proportions are correct. Draw a large circle for the front of the body. Add a circle for the head. Add a circle for the rump area. Draw two curved lines to connect the head to the front body. Draw two lines connecting the front body to the back rump. The top line forms the neck and back; the bottom line is the chest and stomach.

2 More Features

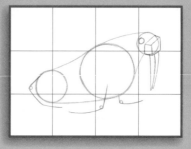

To form the muzzle, draw a rectangular box. Add a circle for an eye. To form the tusks, draw two long, narrow triangles. Draw a line for each leg and foot as shown. Draw a circle for the ankle joints.

3 Adding Details

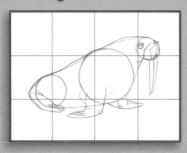

Time to draw organic shapes: the uneven and curvy lines. Draw an eyelid. Draw lines to form the width of the feet. Draw additional curved lines to form the folds around the feet and ankle area, and the toes.

4 Finishing Touches

Erase the geometric shapes that remain visible. Now the walrus looks more lifelike because the organic shapes add form. Draw additional curved lines to form more wrinkles in the legs, belly, chest, and neck areas. Round the lines on the muzzle. Draw short lines to form the whiskers on the muzzle.

TIP:

Use the side of your pencil to create soft, grainy shading. The tip of your pencil will allow you to add denser coloring to your sketch.

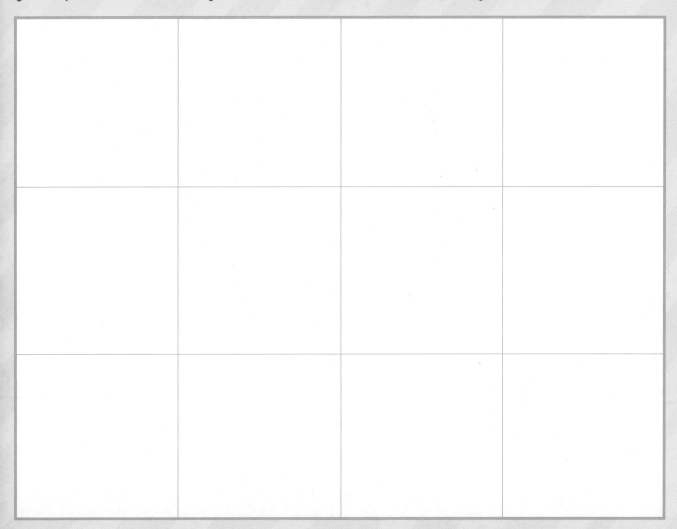

Did you know?
Walruses can live 20 to 30 years in the wild!

HOW TO DRAW AN OCTOPUS

Suggested colors: ●●●●●●

1 Basic Shapes

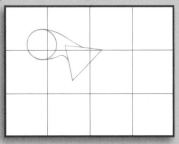

Before you begin, study the size and location of the shapes on the grid so that your proportions are correct. Start with a large circle for the head. Draw a triangle for the body. Draw two curved connecting lines from the head to the body to form the neck.

2 More Features

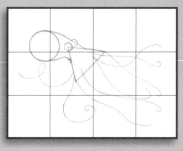

Draw two circles for the eyes. Draw a curved line that follows the path for each of the octopus' tentacles.

3 Adding Details

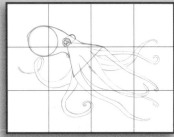

Time to draw organic shapes. Draw an eyelid. Draw more lines to form the width of the tentacles. Be sure to keep looking at the picture of the octopus and the grid to keep your lines curving in the right places, and your proportions correct.

4 Finishing Touches

Erase the geometric shapes that remain visible. Now the octopus is more lifelike because the organic shapes add form. Complete the details around the eyes. Draw lots of circles with smaller circles or dots inside of them for the suction cups on the octopus' tentacles.

IDEA:

Create a scrapbook of inspiration. Collect newspaper and magazine clippings as well as old postcards and photos.

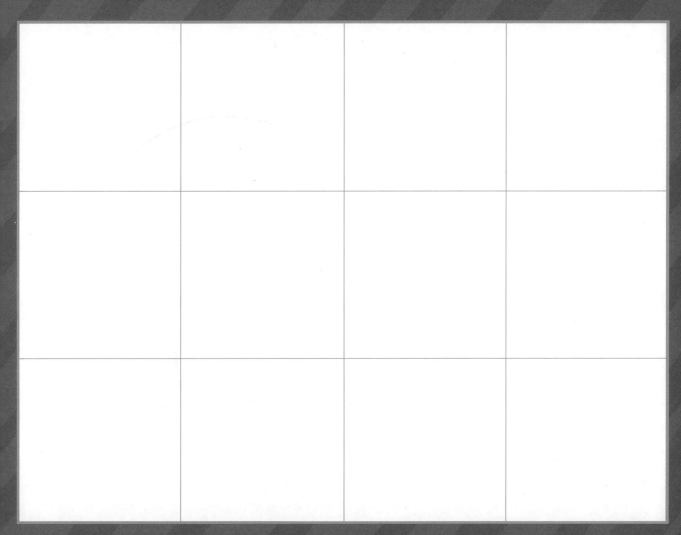

Did you know?

An adult octopus can squeeze through a hole as small as the size of a dime!

HOW TO DRAW A DOLPHIN

Suggested colors:

1 Basic Shapes

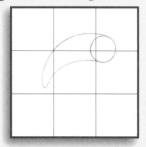

Before you begin, study the size and location of the shapes on the grid so that your proportions are correct. Start by drawing a large circle for the dolphin's head. Then draw a long, curved triangle to form the rest of the body.

2 More Features

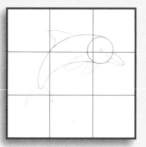

Draw a small circle for the eye. Form the snout with a slightly curved triangle and an interior line for the mouth. Draw a curved, incomplete triangle to form each of the front fins. Draw a triangle for the upper fin on the back. Draw a triangle shape with a curve in it for the tail fin.

3 Adding Details

Time to draw organic shapes. Notice how these lines are uneven and curvy. Draw an eyelid. Draw a smaller shape for the eye pupil. Add a line to form the side of the dolphin's face on the far side. Add a few lines on the body to add shape and depth to the form. On the tail, draw a wavy, almost broken line to define the shape on the edge of the fin.

4 Finishing Touches

Erase any visibly remaining geometric shapes. Now the dolphin is much more lifelike. Draw some additional lines to help separate the lighter belly area from the darker surrounding area. Draw a line to define the upper nasal fold where the snout meets the face. Draw some additional lines around the eye to add expression to the dolphin's face. If you want, add some water falling from the tail.

Did you know?

Dolphins sleep with
one eye open!

HOW TO DRAW A SHARK

Suggested colors:

1 Basic Shapes

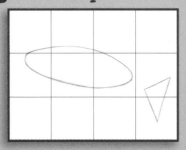

Before you begin, study the size and location of the shapes on the grid so that your proportions are correct. Start by drawing a large, long oval for the shark's body. Then draw a triangle to form the tail.

2 More Features

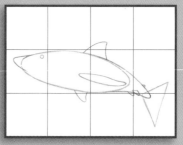

Draw a small circle for the eye. Form the snout with a slightly curved triangle. Draw a curved triangle to form the top and bottom fins. Draw an oval shape with a curve in it for the side fin. Draw two half-ovals for the two flaps on the shark's underside near the tail.

3 Adding Details

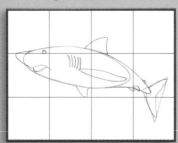

Time to draw organic shapes. Notice how these lines are uneven and curvy. Draw a line to form the eyelid fold and a circle for the eye pupil. Add several curved lines to form the mouth. Add several lines to form gills on the side of the shark's body. On the tail fin, draw an indented line to define the shape on the edge of the fin.

4 Finishing Touches

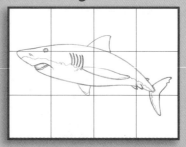

Erase any visibly remaining geometric shapes. Now the shark is much more lifelike. Draw some additional zigzaggy lines to help separate the lighter belly area from the darker surrounding area. Draw a triangle to form the nostril. Draw some additional lines around the body and fins as shown to add form and depth to those shapes.

HOW TO DRAW A STINGRAY

Suggested colors:

1 Basic Shapes

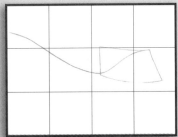

Before you begin, study the size and location of the shapes on the grid so that your proportions are correct. Start by drawing two triangles to form the body of the stingray. Draw a long curved line to form the tail.

2 More Features

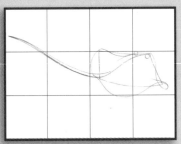

Draw curved lines around the triangle shapes to better define the flowing shape of the stingray's body. Draw additional lines to show folds in the stingray's flaps. Draw two circles for the eyes. Draw a line to form the width of the tail.

3 Adding Details

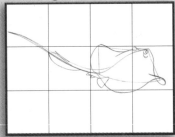

Time to draw organic shapes: the uneven and curvy lines. Draw the additional curved lines to form the bottom fins under the stingray's body. Draw additional lines around the eyes. Draw curved lines to form additional fins on the tail.

4 Finishing Touches

Erase the geometric shapes that remain visible. Now the stingray looks more lifelike because the organic shapes add form. Define the edges of the bottom fins by drawing small folds with short lines. Indicate where the stingray's tail becomes the spine by drawing a bumpy, skipped line.

TIP:

Notice each animal has white highlights in its eyes. When drawing eyes, be sure to make a small circle for the highlight and color in the pupils on the outside.

Did you know?

Stingrays can weigh as much as 790 pounds (358 kg). They can also be more than 6 feet (1.8 m) long!

HOW TO DRAW A WHALE

Suggested colors: ● ● ●

1 Basic Shapes

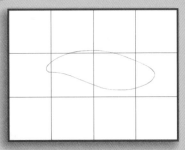

Before you begin, study the size and location of the shapes on the grid so that your proportions are correct. Draw a flattened oval for the whale's body.

2 More Features

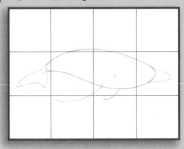

Draw a small circle for the eye. Draw a soft triangle shape for the whale's snout. Draw a triangle for the tail, with connecting lines to the body. Draw curved lines for the front fins.

3 Adding Details

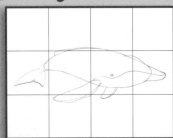

Time to draw organic shapes. Notice how these lines are uneven and curvy. They may be close to, or far away from, the geometric shapes. Draw a wavy line to define the edge of the tail fin and the front fins. Draw a long line from the front of the snout, across the body, and under the eye to form the mouth. Draw a triangular shape on the lower back for the back fin.

4 Finishing Touches

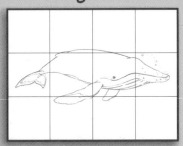

Erase the geometric shapes that remain visible. Now the whale is more lifelike because the organic shapes add form. Draw additional zigzaggy line shapes to help define the darker and lighter color areas on the fins and body of the whale. Draw longer rectangular shapes on the whale's chin. Draw some circles for air bubbles.

IDEA:

Try sketching your own pet from a photograph.
Take the photo at their level for the best angle.

Did you know?

Humpback whales can sing
complicated whale songs that
last as long as 30 minutes!

HOW TO DRAW A BLUE TANG

Suggested colors:

1 Basic Shapes

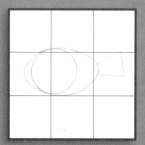

Start by drawing a large circle for the head area. Draw an egg shape around the circle; be sure to use the grid as a guide for the correct size and placement. Draw a triangular shape for the back fin.

2 More Features

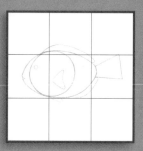

Draw a circle for the eyes. Draw two lines to form the mouth. Draw one long line with a curve at the end to form the upper fin. Draw one long line with a curve at the end to form the lower back fin. Draw a half-oval for the other lower fin. Draw an incomplete triangle to form the side fin.

3 Adding Details

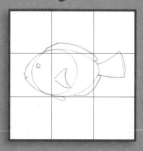

Time to draw organic shapes. Notice how these lines are uneven and curvy. They may be close to, or far away from, the geometric shapes. Draw small, wavy, almost zigzag lines on the edges of the fins. Draw an inner circle for the eye.

4 Finishing Touches

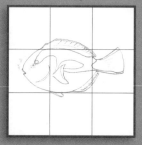

Erase the geometric shapes that remain visible. Now the blue tang is more lifelike because the organic shapes add form. Draw two smaller curved lines to finish forming the upper and lower lips. Add lines around the eye, cheek, and body as shown; these lines form the areas where the color changes. Draw more short lines on the fins as shown to make the folds on the fins. Draw small circles for air bubbles, if desired.

Did you know?

Blue tangs can change the intensity of their skin color from light blue to dark purple!

2

HOW TO DRAW A SEA TURTLE

Suggested colors:

1 Basic Shapes

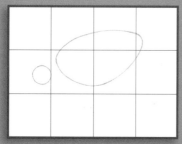

Before you begin, study the size and location of the shapes on the grid so that your proportions are correct. Draw a circle for the head. Draw an egg shape with a flatter bottom for the body shape.

2 More Features

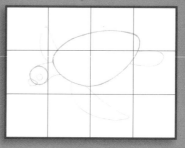

Draw a heart shape for the beak. Draw a circle for the eye. Draw two curved lines to connect the head to the body. Draw three oblong shapes to form the three visible fins.

3 Adding Details

Time to draw organic shapes: the uneven and curvy lines. They are close to, or far away from, the geometric shapes. Draw an oval with pointed ends to refine the eye shape. Draw a curved line to form the lower edge of the top beak. Draw zigzag lines to form the edges of the sea turtle's fins. Draw angular shapes to form the scales all over the turtle's shell. Use the grid and drawing to help you make them the right size and shape.

4 Finishing Touches

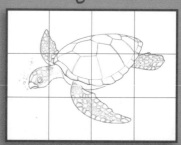

Erase the geometric shapes that remain visible. Now the sea turtle looks more lifelike because the organic shapes add form. Draw interior lines on the turtle shell to define the breaks between the panels. Draw lots of angular shapes on each fin and on the sea turtle's head. This pattern adds texture to the drawing. Draw some additional lines on the beak and around the eye and neck to add more shape. Draw circles for air bubbles.

IDEA:

When you are more confident in drawing, experiment with different drawing media such as chalk, crayons, pastels and pen, and ink.

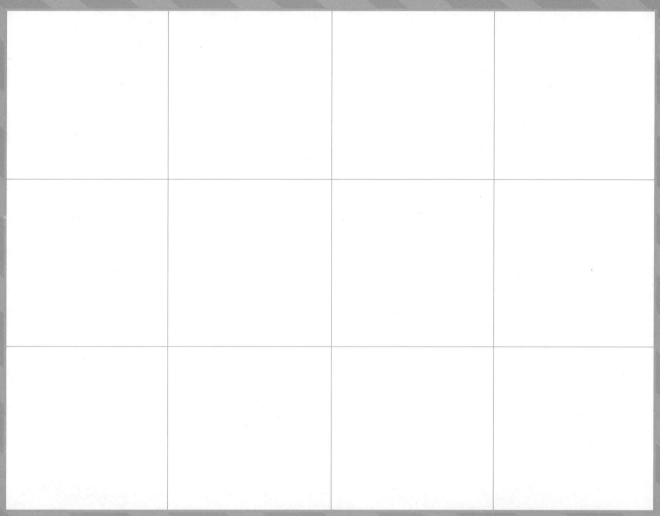

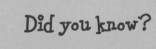

Did you know?

Sea turtles (like other turtles)
have no teeth!

Time to practice drawing in color!

Use the following grid sheets to practice sketching and coloring using the four-step grid system. Try drawing the twelve animals in this book and many more!

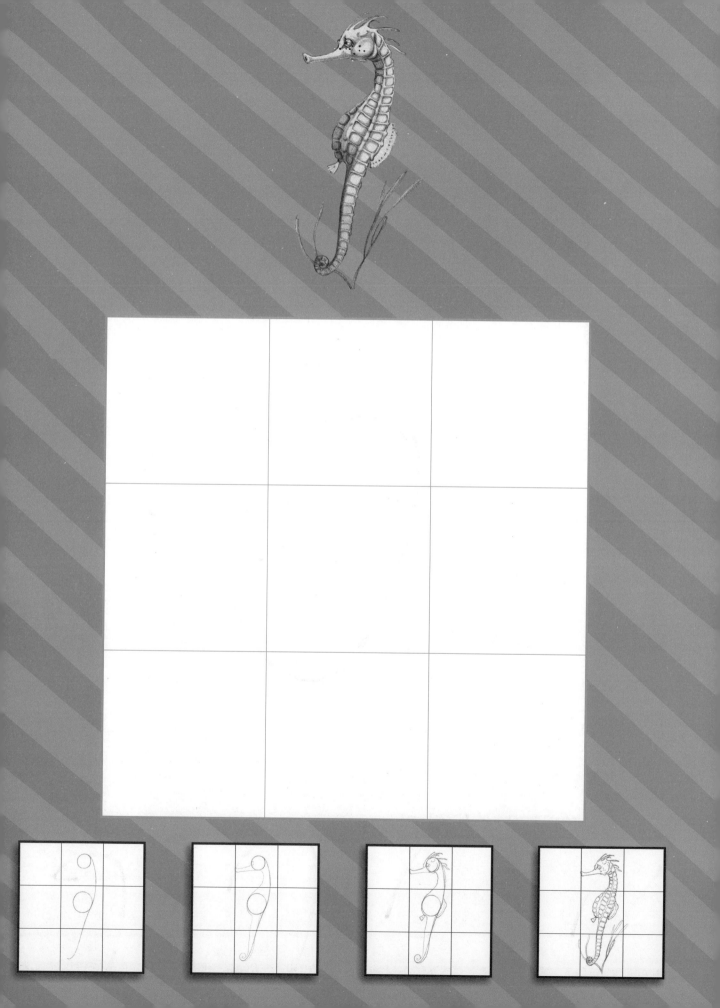

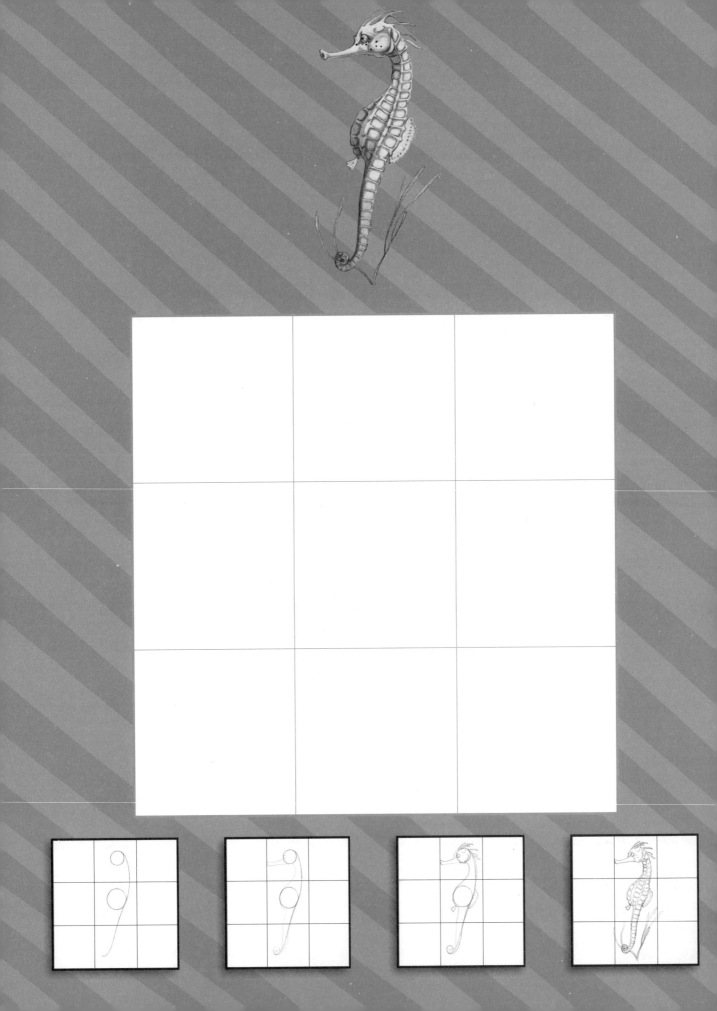

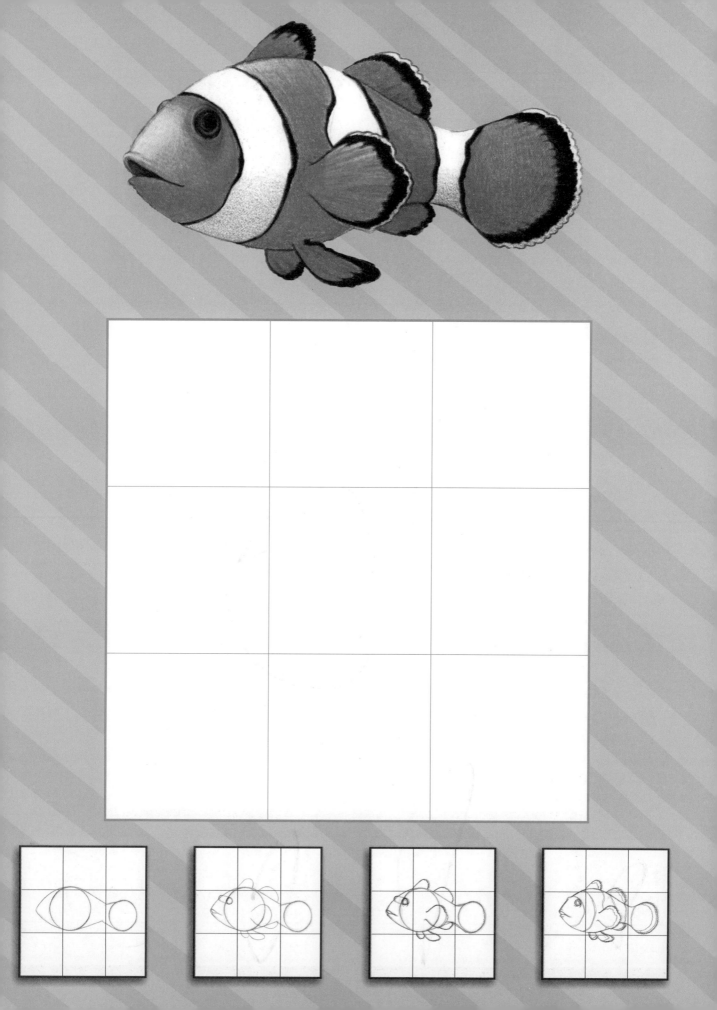

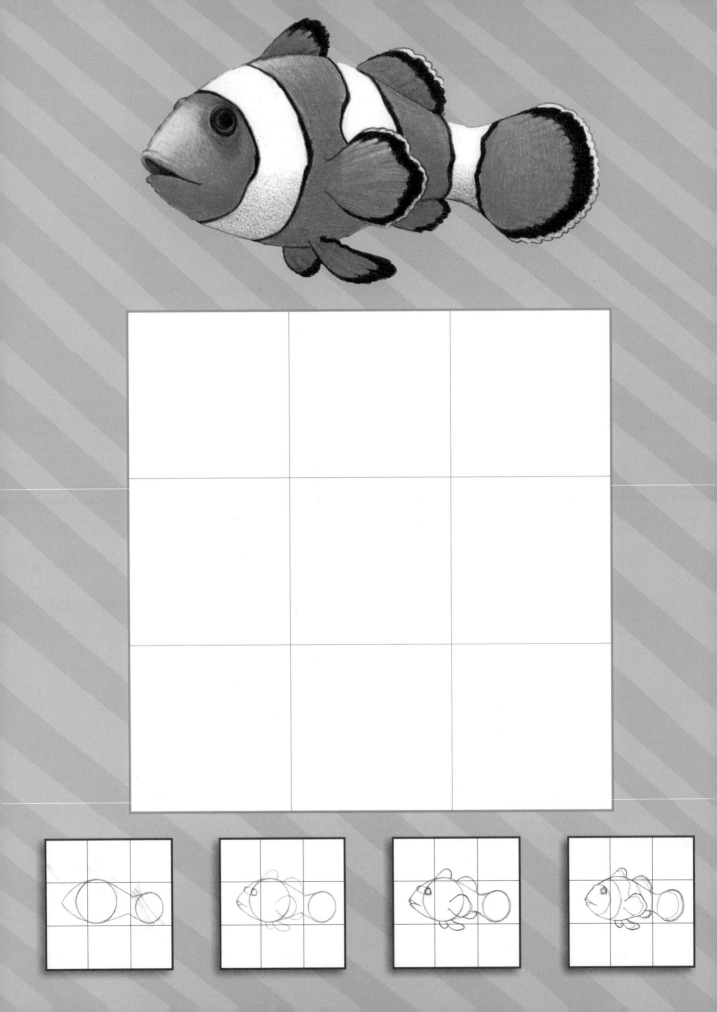

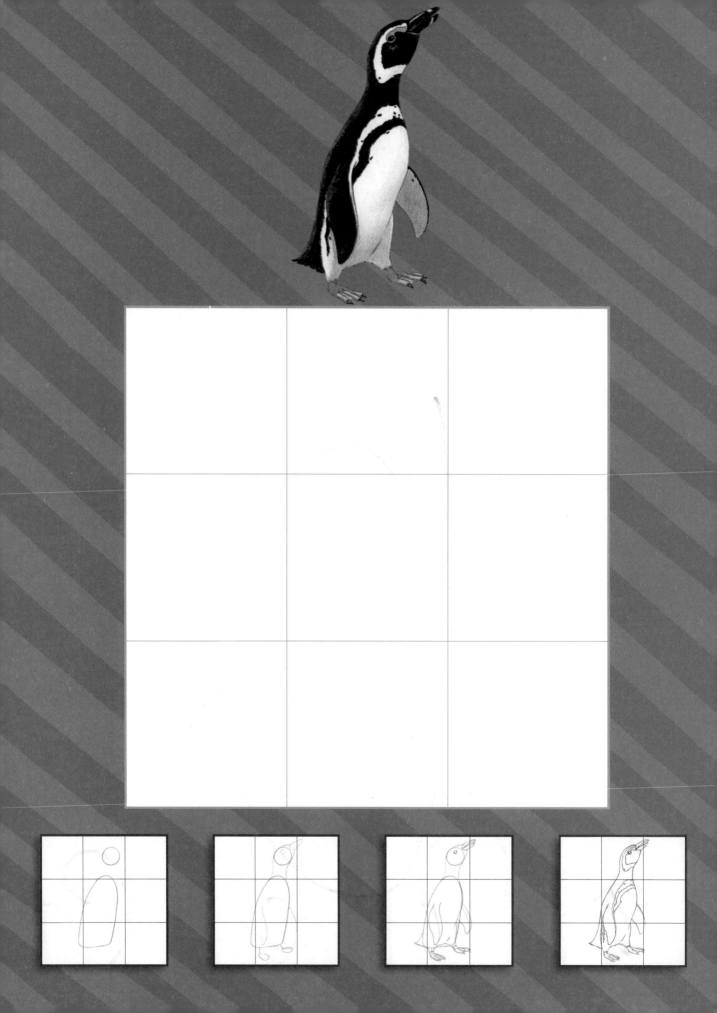

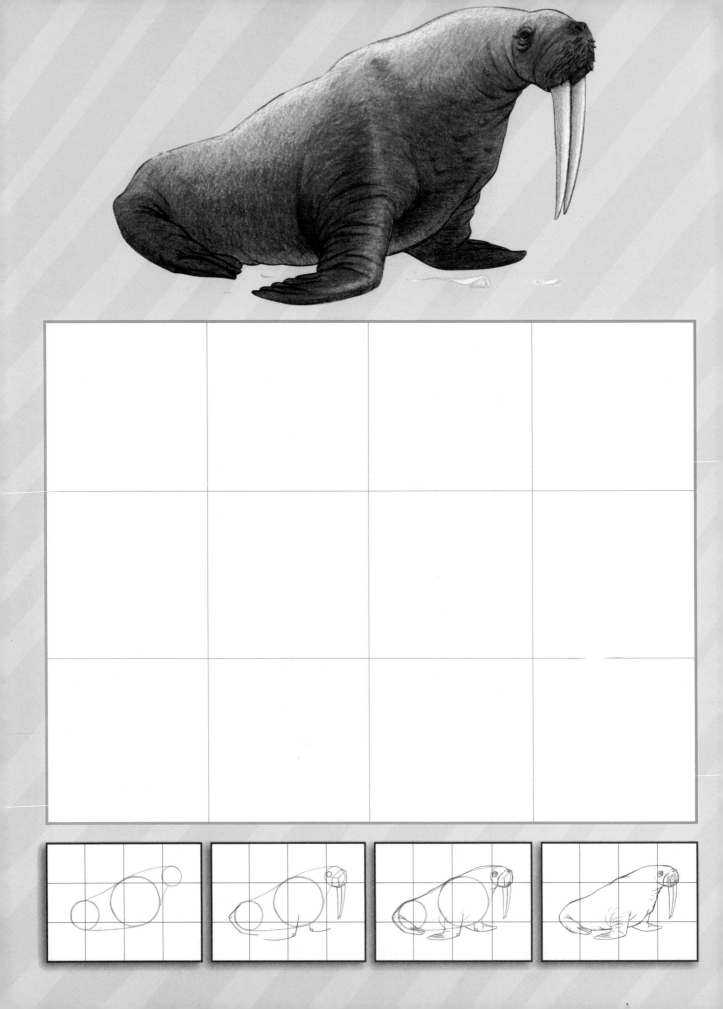

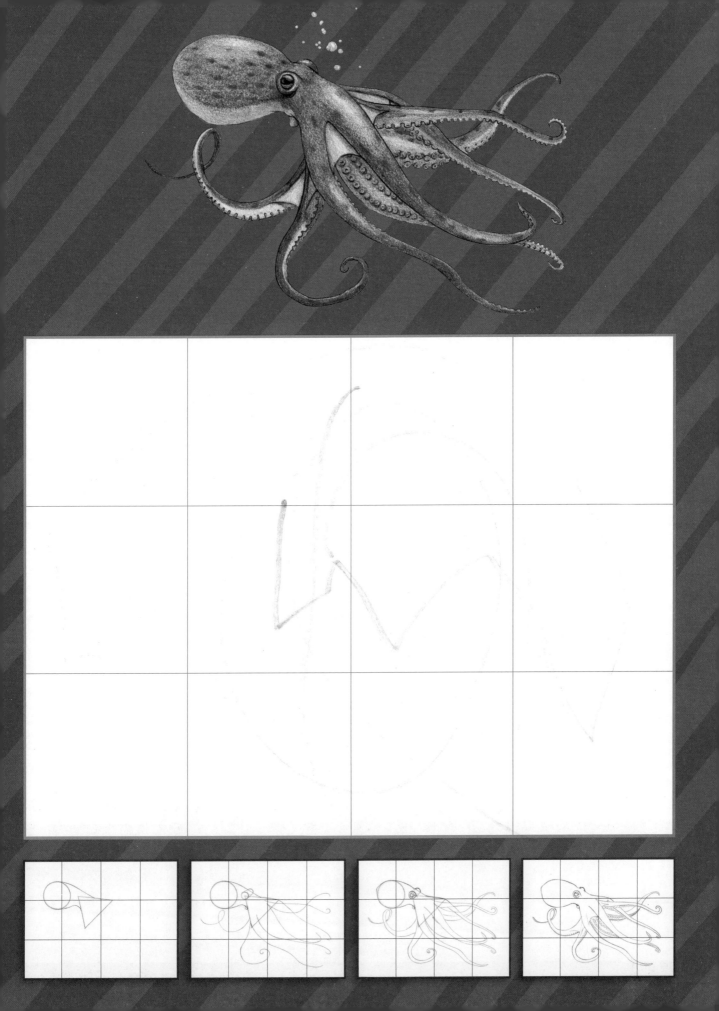

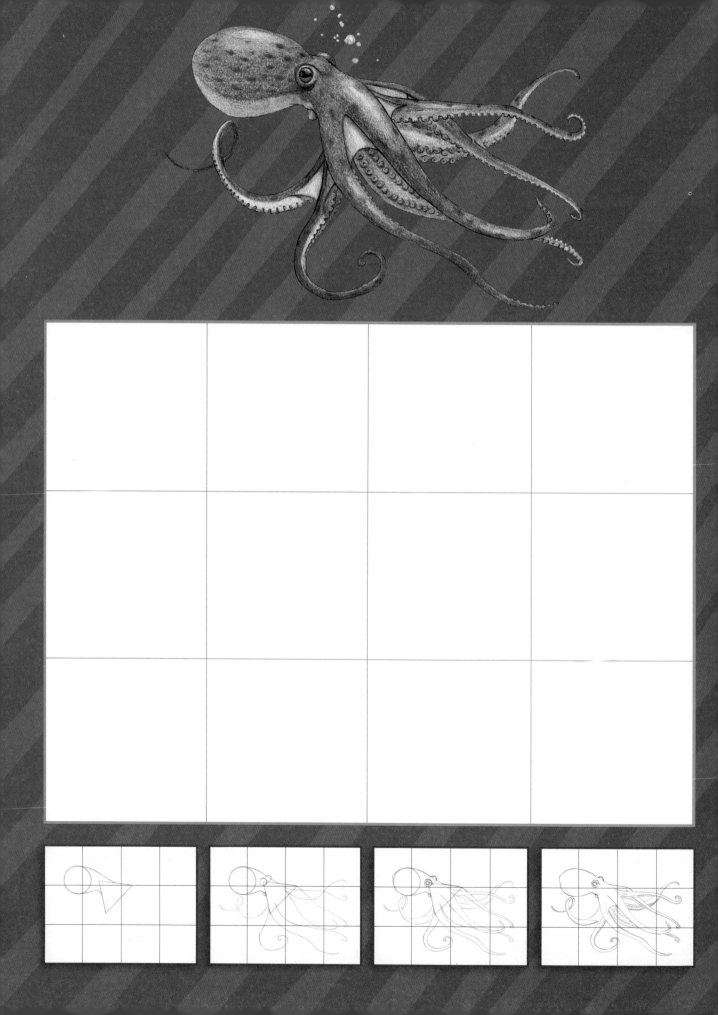

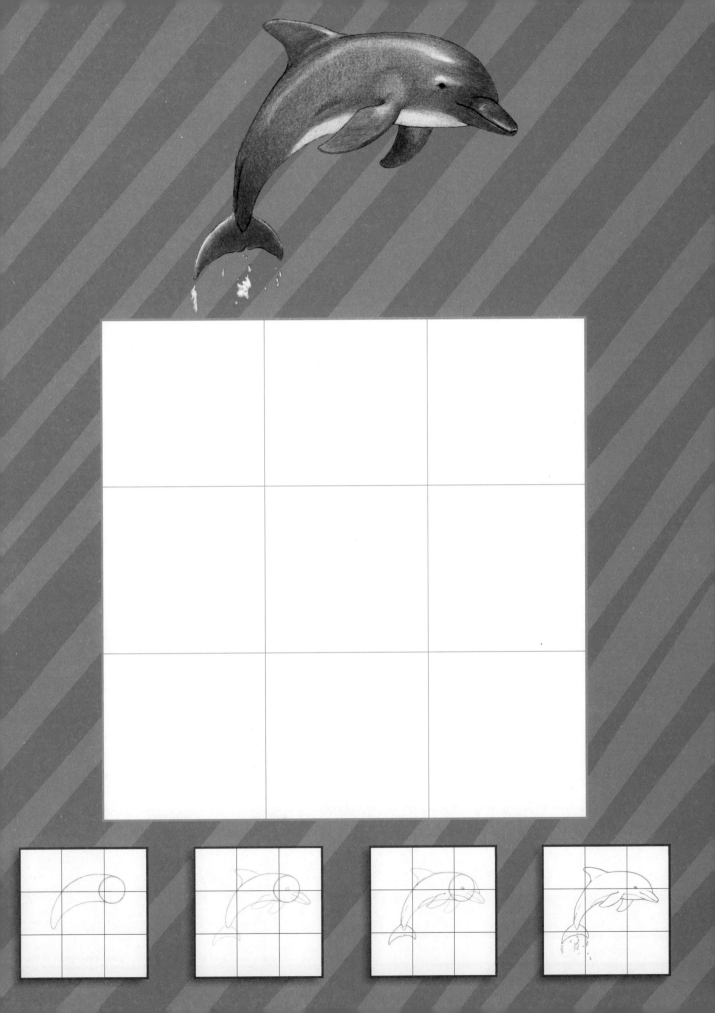

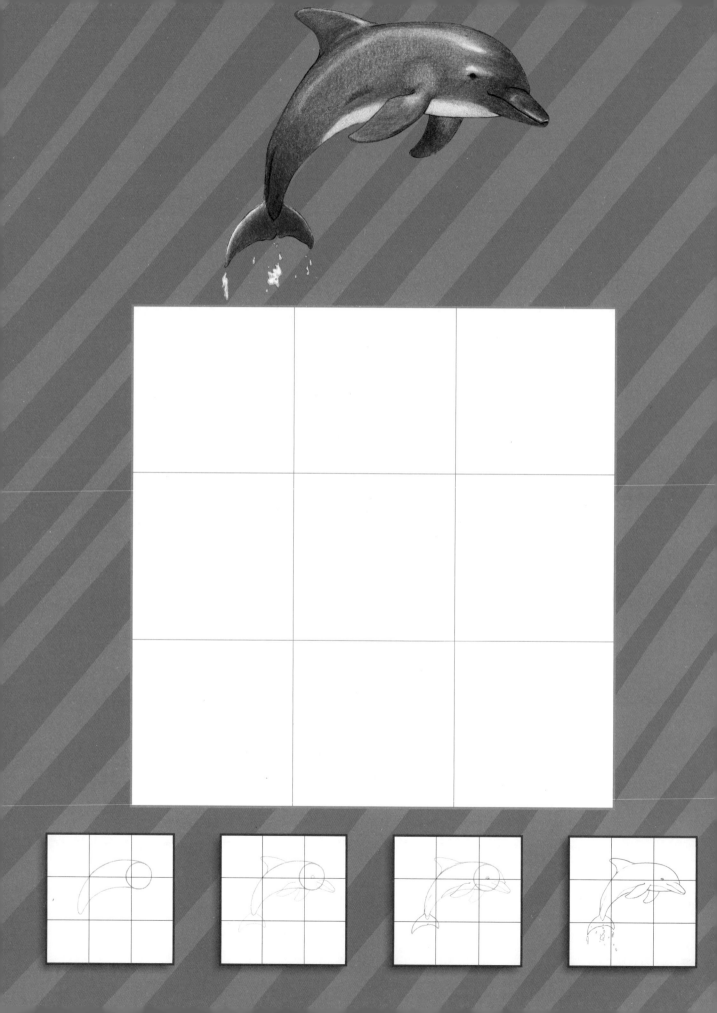

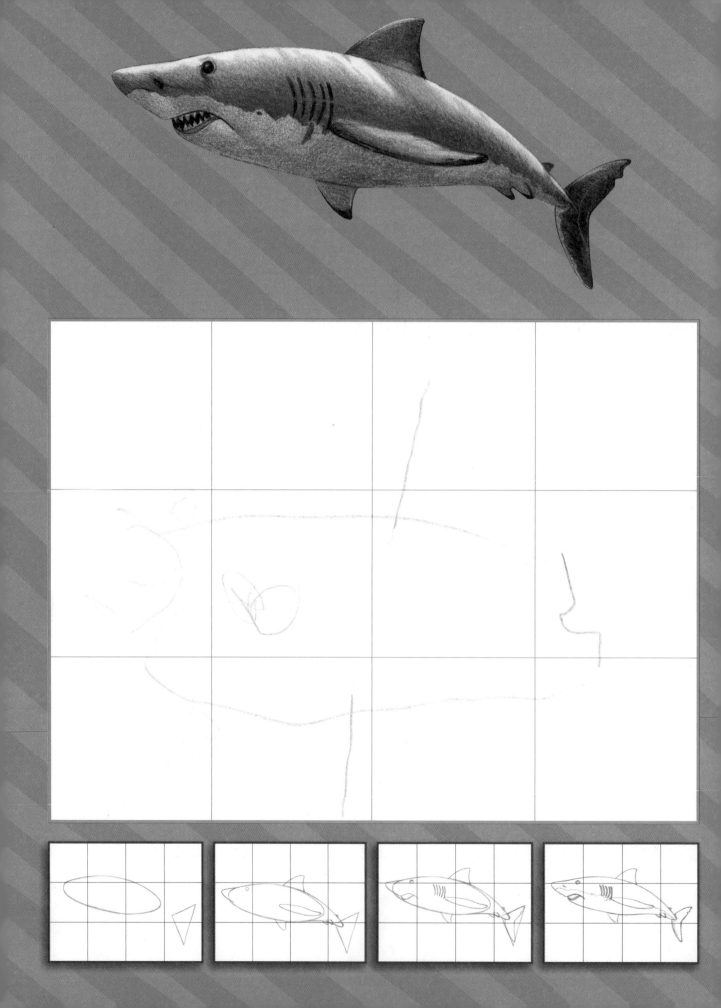

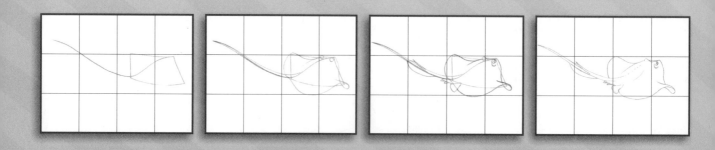

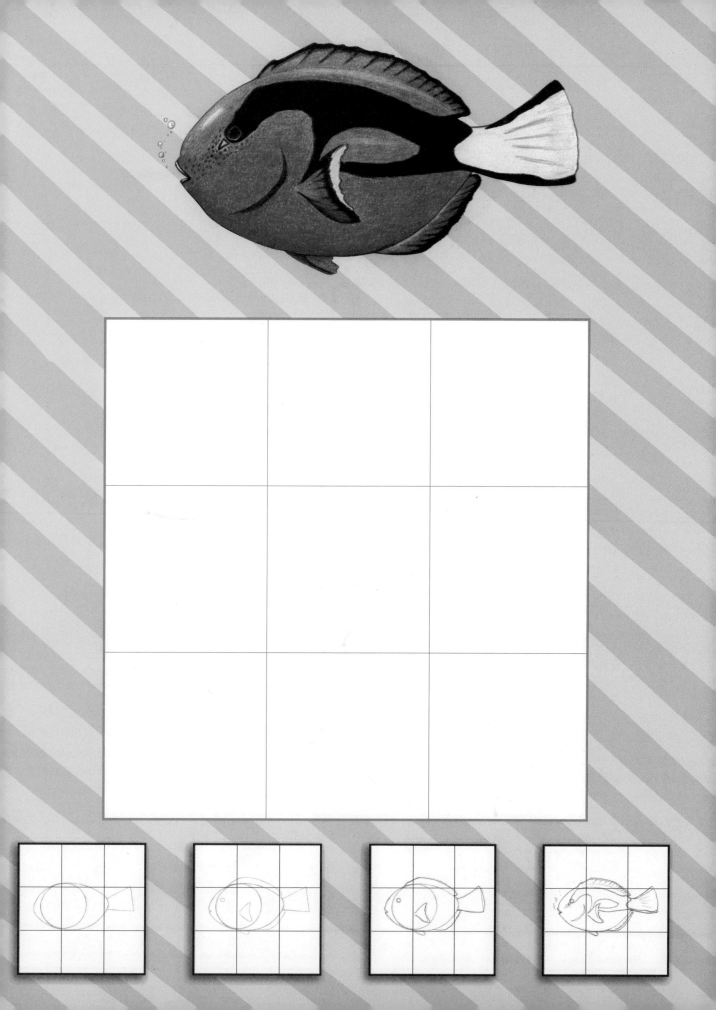

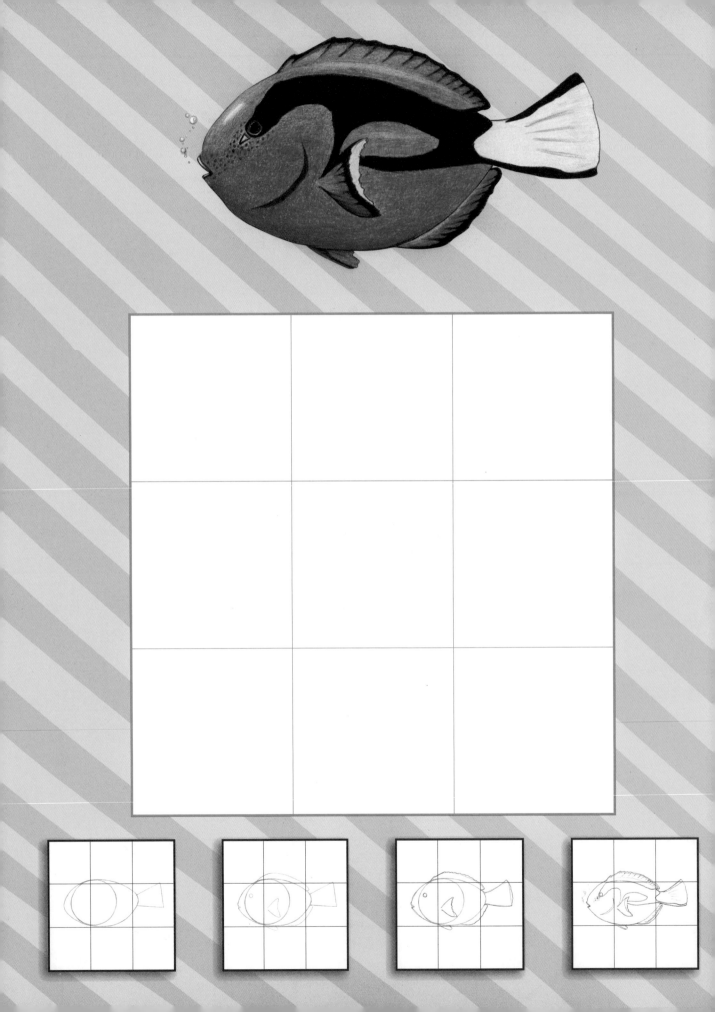

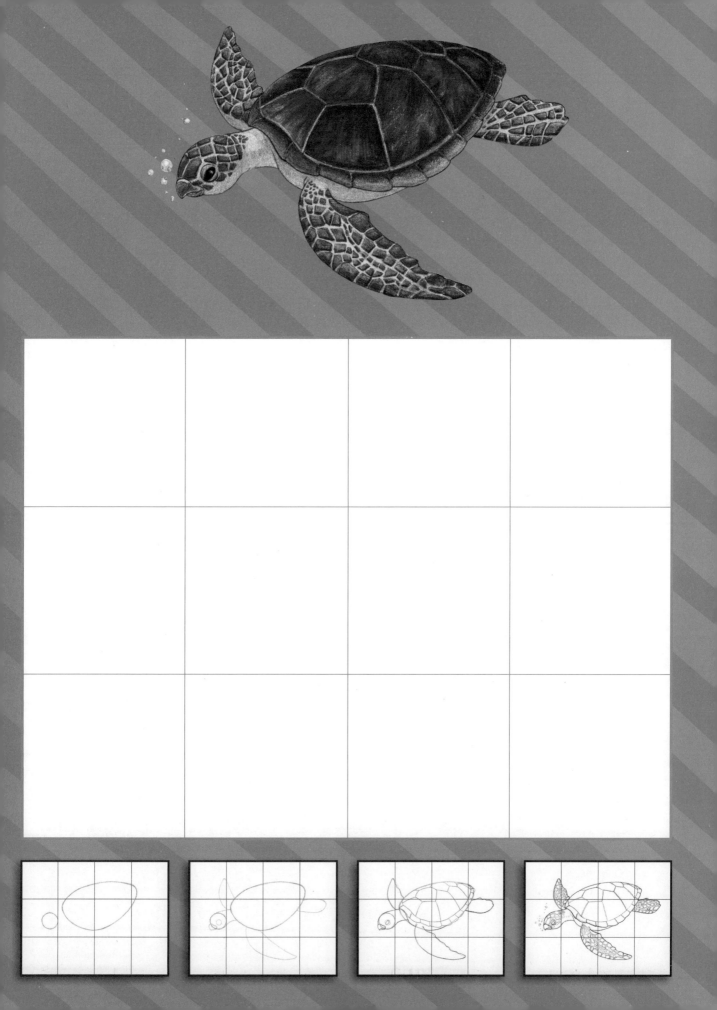

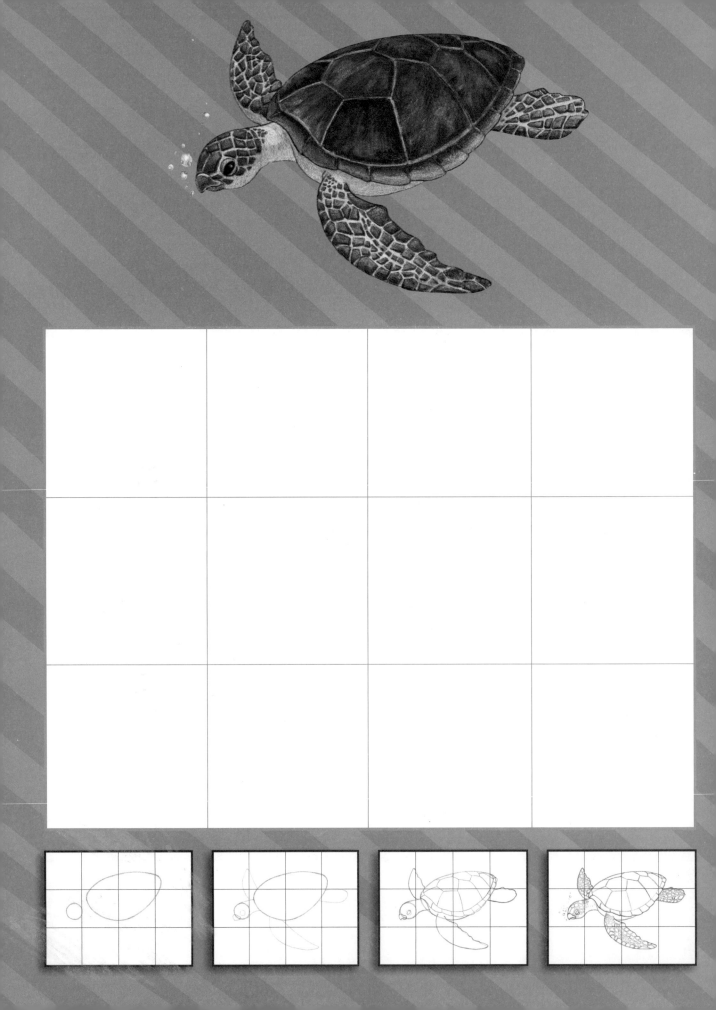

Now that you have learned the simple step-by-step process of drawing with a grid, try to create more realistic sketches from photographs of ocean animals.

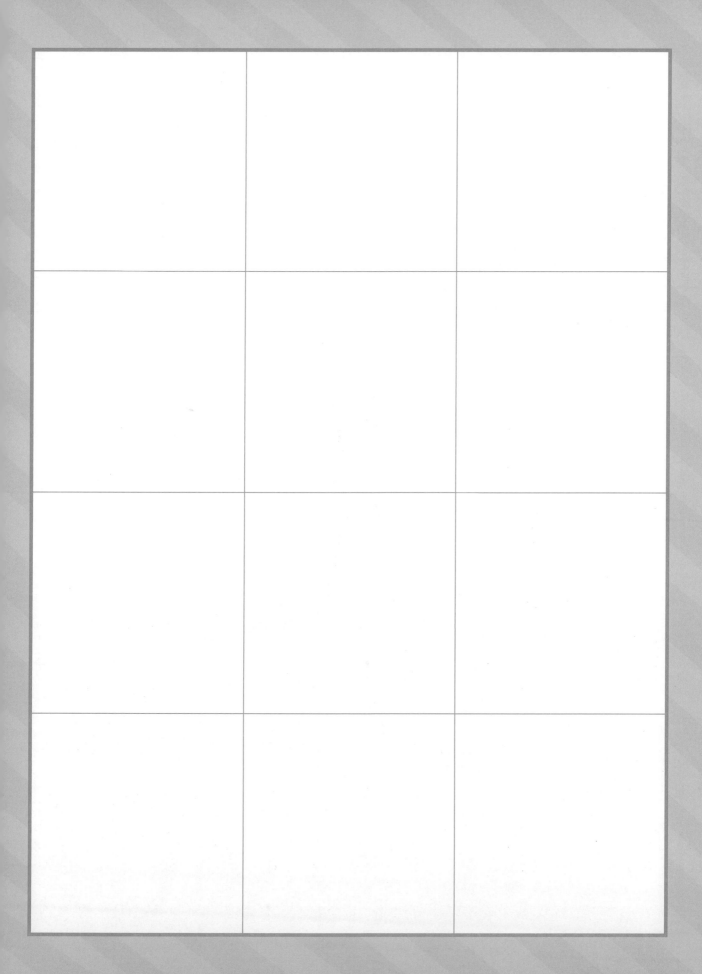

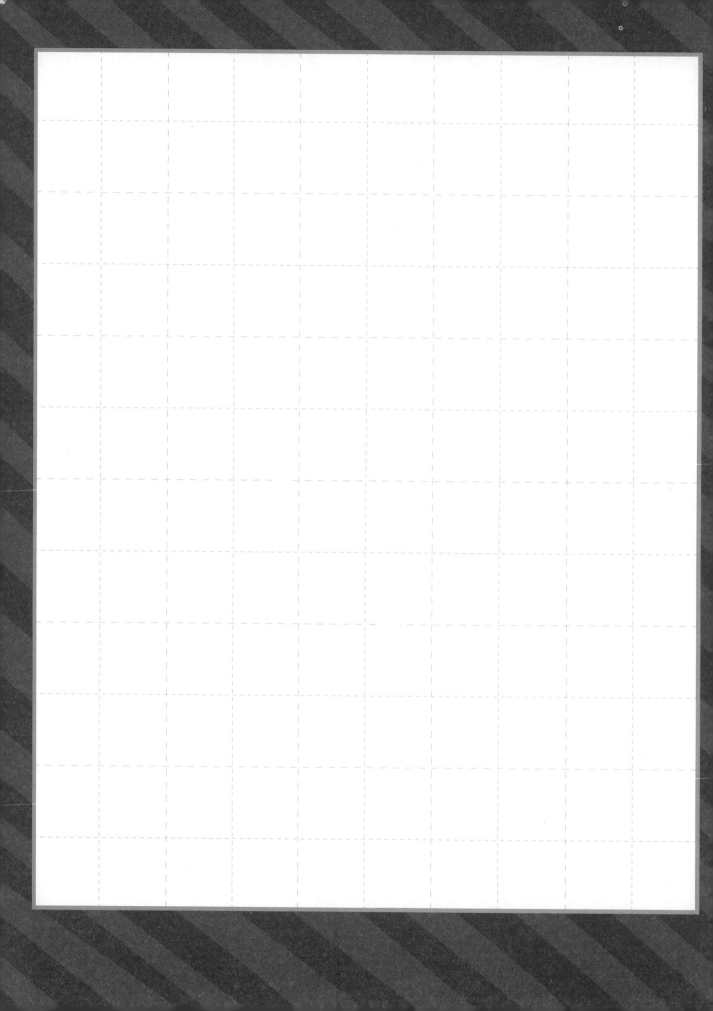